Classroom Management

Comprehensive Guide To Outstanding Classroom Management and Higher Level Behavior

(2014 Edition)

By KJ O'Hara

ISBN: 978-1499251876

Published by Antic Mind
102 Dudwell Lane, Halifax, UK. HX30SH
All enquiries to publisher@anticmind.com

ANTIC MIND

Contents

Introduction

For many teachers the term 'classroom management' basically means keeping the children well behaved, making the classroom quiet enough for learning to take place and dealing with troublesome students. In recent years, however, the bar has been raised. Globally, new ideas about pedagogy and the resulting changes in classroom practice means that there are new expectations of the teacher when it comes to managing student behavior in the classroom.

Today, a classroom full of quiet, compliant students is not good enough. Instead, school leaders expect students' behavior to contribute to the learning. They should be enthusiastic, resilient, genuinely engaged and co-operating well enough to solve problems together and help each other progress.

Of course, none of this is possible if the children are misbehaving in the first place. The aim of this book, therefore, is two-fold: firstly it will explain how teachers can establish and maintain good classroom behavior and secondly it will show you techniques which you can use to: build up resilience; make your students more enthusiastic; better engage them in the tasks you set; and finally, how to get them cooperating to solve problems and help each other learn.

Before we look at any of the techniques, we need to remember one simple thing: just as teachers have to learn the skills of classroom management, children need to learn the skills of the classroom too. In order to achieve this we will have to teach students these skills and nurture their development.

This is particularly true for students in their first few years of education, but all students still have things to learn about behavior, social interaction, working together and meeting expectations. Whilst they may know about many of these things, their skill in applying that knowledge during lessons may need developing.

Preparing for the New Academic Year

Getting organized for day one

First impressions count. If you turn up on the first day of term having to arrange everything in an ad hoc manner it will be clearly evident to your class that you are disorganized. Below are some essential things you should do to help you establish good classroom management from day one.

1)   Use data to arrange seating plans

The classroom belongs to you and from the outset you need to let the students know that you are in charge of who sits where. Doing this is one of the key factors in establishing your authority as a teacher.

If you have a brand new class, you need to use any data you already have to arrange seating so that it is best for learning to take place. Once you have got to know the individual students better you can always make changes later, but letting them sit where they want, particularly on the first day of the school year, does not set a strong message of who is in charge.

Get the seating plan arranged in advanced so that, from the moment they arrive, you seat the children where you want them.

2)   Prepare behavior expectation displays

Before the first day of term make sure that you have the classroom rules clearly visible on the walls of your room.

It is absolutely essential that these are fully in line with the whole school behavior policy, so if you are new to a school make sure you know what the policy is.

Many schools have a pre-designed classroom rules poster printed or available to print so that there is consistency across the school. Before you create your own poster, check to see if one of these is available.

Again, do this in advance as you will need to refer to it on the first day of term.

If you do create your own rules poster it needs to be:

- clearly written and explicit
- large enough to be seen everywhere
- written in student friendly language
- the rules should be few in number (no more than 4 or 5, too many becomes confusing)
- written using positive language e.g. 'I will let other people work without interrupting them,' rather than 'Don't disrupt others.'

3) Print out class photographs

Many schools have data systems which allow you to see the photographs of the class you are teaching. If these are available, get a print out and keep it on your desk. They will be very useful in helping you get to know the names of the children and address them by their name.

If you don't have access to photographs, then stick a copy of the seating plan to your desk so you can look at who is sitting where to help you remember the names.

4) If you are new to a school, fully familiarize yourself with the school behavior policy and procedures

I can't underestimate the importance of this. All schools have a policy which explains how rewards and sanctions will be applied and in what circumstances. This will be backed up by a set of procedures for staff which you need to follow to ensure that policy is put into place.

It is absolutely vital to the success of that policy that all the procedures are followed by all staff in a consistent way. Failure to do this can lead to discipline within the entire school breaking down. I have seen what happens when it does and its impact upon learning, staff and pupil morale and the progress students make is devastating.

You need to make sure from the outset that you apply that policy and follow those procedures in your lessons. When you do this there can be no come back from the students because what you are doing is what everyone else is doing.

If you are in a school where children move from teacher to teacher for different lessons, it means that students know exactly what is expected of them in every lesson and because every teacher follows those procedures they perceive it as fair.

Using your own disciplinary procedures leaves children feeling unsure about what to expect and how to behave. They may perceive you as being unfair if you are over strict and weak if you are not as strict.

Meeting Your New Class for the First Time

1)   Adopting the right tone

There are three types of disciplinary stances that a teacher can take:

- the ruthless dictator
- firm but fair
- the friendly mentor

The only choice here is the second one. A ruthless dictator will not get the children on their side, the students will do things out of fear but won't give their respect and consequently the teacher won't get the best out of them. You may achieve compliance and a quiet classroom but the fearful environment will restrict the development of higher level behavior.

The friendly mentor will be loved by some and walked all over by others. Many students will perceive overfriendliness as a weakness and seek to exploit it to disrupt lessons and get away with doing as little work as possible. Being too friendly can cause problems when you need to exert order in a classroom or deal with bad behavior. This kind of management style can lead to every lesson being a challenge and can make the teacher's working life unbearable.

The firm but fair teacher adheres consistently to the school behavioral policy. They will not let students get away with rule breaking or disruption but are fair in how they administer discipline. The fairness and consistency will earn the teacher respect and the firmness with which they apply the rules will ensure that behavior is generally good. It still leaves room for you to be humorous and have good personal relationships with the students, but there is a clear line which the students know cannot be crossed.

2)   Don't smile until Christmas

Not to be taken literally, the saying *'Don't smile until Christmas'* originated in British schools where the academic year starts in September. It basically implies that you need to be at your strictest when you start teaching a class for the first time.

The advantages of doing this are:

- It quickly establishes your authority
- enables you to firmly embed rules and routines
- clearly signals to students the nature of your relationship to them
- allows you to get to know all the students well before you can decide whether to be a little less strict or whether you need to maintain the strictness

Over the years I've been called on many times to intervene in classrooms where teachers are struggling with behavior because when they first started teaching a new class they had adopted an over friendly approach. Doing this created a set of behavioral expectations within that classroom which the teacher, when they really needed to, found very difficult to turn around.

Starting off by being very strict and then easing off once you have got your rules embedded and established good relationships is much easier than doing it the other way around.

3)   Explain the rules, expectations and routines

When you first begin to teach a class, the main rules, expectations and routines should be clearly visible on the classroom walls. This acts as a constant reminder to the students and enables you to refer to them when the need occurs.

The very first lesson you teach to a class should be about those rules, expectations and routines. The lesson should cover:

- what the rules, expectations and routines are
- why those rules, expectations and routines are important
- what the rewards and sanctions will be for following or not following them

In addition, there is also the need to discuss your own specific rules, expectations and routines. For example, if the school rule is, 'You must not do anything to endanger the health and safety of yourself or others,' a physical education teacher might discuss why not to throw javelins in the direction of others or a science teacher might want to explain the need to wear safety glasses.

Make sure that as part of your high expectations of good behavior that you insist that students have good manners towards all people, staff and students alike, when in your care. You should also model this behavior yourself.

Cardinal Sins

There are several things that things that teachers should never do. Here I have explained what they are and why we shouldn't do them.

1)   Never hit a student – even in jest

I think it goes without saying that actually hitting a student is wrong. It is assault and will no doubt lead you to prosecution, losing your job and probably being banned from teaching.

However, some teachers, whilst they wouldn't dream of hitting a student to hurt them have got themselves into very hot water simply by jokingly hitting or physically manhandling a student.

It may be done even as a sign of friendliness, but if it gets talked about, passed on to parents or if the student doesn't realize it's done in jest then it can be treated just as seriously as a genuine assault. Don't do it.

Generally speaking, don't touch students. If you do, then putting a hand on their shoulder is the best place.

2)   Getting into a flashpoint situation

Flashpoint situations, simply speaking, are argumentative confrontations between a teacher and a student. They generally occur when teachers let their own anger or frustration get the better of them and they respond in the wrong way. Always remember, you are the professional and adult in the room. No matter how angry and annoying the student is, you must deal with the matter in a calm and controlled manner.

Without a doubt, flashpoint situations are potentially one of the most dangerous behavioral situations that can happen. At the extreme, there is the risk of the teacher making inappropriate comments or even being physically aggressive towards the student, which can lead to disciplinary or even legal action against them. There is also the risk of the student lashing out, physically, against the teacher or even other students. The more aggressive a teacher is in their response, the more likely this will happen.

A further set of consequences is that flashpoints: compromise the teacher's authority in the classroom; prevent learning from taking place; and have a destructive effect on the teacher's relationship with the whole class. On several occasions I've had to permanently move teachers from one teaching group to another because a flashpoint situation with a single student had caused irreparable damage to the teacher's working relationship with the entire group.

Thankfully, flashpoints are rare occurrences, but I would say that many teachers' understanding of how bad they are comes from experience of being in them. Even mild flashpoints can rob you of a few nights' sleep and take you weeks to rebuild the relationships with the class. It can also have a serious impact on your own confidence as a teacher.

If you are ever in a situation where you genuinely feel angry with a student and think this might lead you to act in a confrontational way, then there is a simple solution: immediately remove the student from the classroom. Send them to someone more senior or put them in the corridor and call for someone to remove them straight away.

If they are extremely confrontational and refuse to leave then, for safeguarding reasons, take yourself and the rest of the students out of the classroom and call for a senior leader to remove them.

Always remember, in the classroom, you are the adult and the professional; no matter how angry you might feel at a student's behavior, the expectation is that you will deal with this in a calm and sensible way.

3)   Don't ridicule the students

Belittling students, even in jest, is another thing teachers must not do. You can belittle them in several ways:

- being sarcastic
- saying negative things about them
- comparing them negatively to other students
- comparing them negatively to their siblings
- making a joke at their expense

Doing any of the above can have a negative effect not only upon your relationship with that child but also with their peers. It can have a lasting influence on how they behave and work in your classes. It can also result in parental complaints about you.

Ridiculing students can cause:

- resentment
- demotivation
- loss of self esteem
- reluctance to behave well

In addition to these, it also sends a message that belittling people is acceptable and this can lead to bullying.

4)   Don't punish the whole class for the misdemeanors of a few

The aim of a good disciplinarian is to be firm but fair. To be fair, one should only punish those who have broken the rules. Sometimes, however, when we have a bad lesson and there is a lot of disruption by a lot of students, we can be tempted to punish the whole class.

There will be some students in that class, however, who will have done as they were expected and it would not be fair at all to punish them because the rest of the class was naughty. Don't do it.

Only punish those students who you have caught in the act and if some have behaved worse than others sanction them according to the severity of their actions.

Students have an excellent grasp of fairness and a great appreciation of those who are fair. They will respect you all the more if you show this by not blanket-bombing the entire class for the action of others.

Similarly, by letting the children who have behaved well go without punishment you set them up as examples of good behavior to the rest of the class. If you punish the ones who have been good, you risk making them resent you and are sowing the seeds of further problems in the future. If you lose the respect of the better students the chance of winning over the ones who misbehave is much more difficult to achieve.

If you are in a situation where there are many students in the class not doing as you request, you can, by all means, halt the lesson and speak to the whole group about their behavior and your expectations. This is fine; punishing the whole group is not.

Essentials for Excellent Classroom Behavior

So far we have looked at why we should:

- prepare in advance
- start off in the year with the correct tone
- establish clear classroom rules
- follow school policy and procedures
- never break 'cardinal sins'

The next part of the book will look at the essentials of behavior management. These are the principles on which the foundations of good classroom management are laid and which can lead to excellent behavior even with the most challenging of students.

1)   Model good behavior

Many students spend more time in the company of teachers than they do with their own parents. Many teenagers spend much of their time out of school either socializing with friends or hiding in their bedrooms, whilst many younger children have only a few hours at home before they go to bed. This means that our own behavior can have a significant influence on our students – particularly if we are an elementary teacher who spends all day with the same group of students. It is obvious, then, that we have a clear responsibility to our students, their parents and society as a whole, to ensure that any influence we do have is positive.

From a behavior management perspective it is important that we model the behavior that we expect our students adopt. This means being:

- polite and well mannered
- sympathetic and empathetic
- a good listener
- fair
- level headed
- resilient

There's nothing worse than that hypocritical feeling you get when you tell a student off for doing something and they reply with, 'Well, you do it!'

Whether it is something trivial like stopping a student from drinking in a class as you take a sip from your coffee cup or shouting at a student for shouting, the failure to model the required behavior yourself makes implementing expected behavior much harder.

As the adult in the room, students will look to your behavior as an example of what adults do. There will also be an expectation, from them, that because you are the adult, everything you do will be acceptable. They will do what you do because this is what responsible adults do. If what you do is wrong, they will still see this as being acceptable.

Of course, we all do things which are not good examples to others. Whilst we try our best to model good behavior in lessons we will make mistakes – it's what makes us human. As a good role model, when we do, we should let the children know we have done wrong, apologize for it and then change our behavior in future. This way we also teach the children how to do the same.

2)   Be consistent

Being consistent requires quite a lot of self-discipline and can be difficult to maintain. Lack of consistency, however, is one of the biggest causes of poor behavior in classrooms.

What do we mean when we say 'consistent'?

To be consistent we need to apply the school behavior policy and follow its procedures:

- at all times
- in the same manner with our classes
- in the same manner with individual students

Failure to be consistent can cause different problems depending on how you are being inconsistent. I will discuss each of the bullet points above separately to discuss how each type of inconsistency is caused and the problems it creates.

Not being consistent at all times

In my last school we had a policy where if a student disrupted the lesson once, teachers were to give a warning. On the next occasion they misbehaved they received a level 1 sanction: their name was written on a board on the classroom wall and a tick put against it. If they received a second tick, their level 2 sanction was a 'talking to' at the end of a lesson. A level 3 sanction was a lunch time detention and the incident was logged on the school's database. A level 4 sanction would result in their removal from class, an hour's detention after school and their parents being contacted.

As a leadership group, we scrutinized the data that was being logged. We noticed that teachers applied the rules consistently at the beginning of the school year with only a small number of students getting level 3 and 4 sanctions.

After several weeks there was a tailing off of the numbers of level 3 and 4 sanctions being recorded by staff. A few weeks after that, however, and we noticed that some teachers began to make huge increases in the number of students they were sanctioning.

The reason for this was that whilst all teachers started the year off with every intention to be consistent, once things were going well with a class they slackened off. Instead of putting ticks on the board, they just kept warning students. As a result, a student could be told off numerous times in a lesson without getting their name on the board at all and with no sanction being given.

This, however, caused two problems which worked together to cause real issues for the teacher. Firstly, by continually warning instead of following the clearly staged discipline procedure, the teacher was sending out the message to the students that they could keep on disrupting as the only consequence would be another warning. This led to a gradual increase in misbehavior which eventually forced the teachers to readopt the procedures. However, as they had stopped using them, the students reacted negatively when they were reintroduced. As a result, the numbers of students getting level 3 and 4 in these classes dramatically rose – in many cases way above where they had been before the teacher slackened off.

The way to succeed with applying school behavior policy is to think of it like toothpaste. If you use it every day without fail, you reduce the chances of needing dental work. The problem is that some teachers perceive it to be more like a dentist's drill: a tool they only need to use when drastic action is needed. Lack of consistency in applying the policy confuses the students, it blurs the boundary between what is and isn't acceptable in your classroom and leads to significant increases in poor behavior. The students will misbehave when it is not used and be resentful and argumentative when you suddenly reintroduce it.

One thing that makes consistency difficult for teachers is that sometimes our phenomenal workload just gets in the way. Finding two minutes to log an incident, having the time to speak to the student at the end of one lesson when there's another about to begin and the many other things we need to do in a day, make keeping it up difficult and it's easy to slip.

In the end, however, for your own sanity as well as for the benefit of the class, putting behavior as a priority, even when it's not been a major problem, is in your long term interests.

Being consistent in manner

We all have off days and it can be all too easy when these happen to be inconsistent in how we apply school rules and sanction students. What was so insignificant and trivial yesterday when the sun was shining and everything was hunky dory, can today, when your car broke down and your boss just lambasted you, seems enormous. As a result, we can let students off for something on Monday and then sanction them for it on Tuesday.

This leaves students not knowing where they stand as far as the rules go in your room. The lack of clarity is confusing, it makes them uncomfortable and you are likely to see them react with, 'You let me do it yesterday!'

To be effective, you need to be consistent both ways. Don't let them off because you've just been promoted and don't punish them just because your own kids had a tantrum before you left home this morning.

Being consistent with different students

One of the responsibilities I had as a senior leader was to remove students who'd been given level 4 sanctions from lessons. When you do this you begin to pick up on certain things that happen around the school.

On Thursday mornings I was always called to the same class to remove the same student – and always within 5 minutes of the lesson starting.

The first thing that goes through your head as you take the message on the walkie-talkie and make your way over to the room is that this student is having yet another bad lesson. If they can't last more than 5 minutes into the school day, then something is seriously wrong.

In this case, though, it was the teacher at fault. The student was by no means an angel and, more than likely, would have disrupted the teacher's lesson as it progressed. Indeed, it was the student's poor behavior in the past that had caused the teacher to be extremely inconsistent. So fed up was the teacher of this student's disruption, that they were no longer treating him in the same way as everyone else. It was as if the teacher spent the first few minutes of the lesson looking for something, no matter how trivial, to give the student a warning for.

The result, of course, was that the student would react. It usually went something like this (the name of the student has been changed):

John is having a conversation with another student.

Teacher, ignoring the other student, 'John stop talking, that's your warning.'

'It wasn't just me.'

'You've talked again, that's level 1.'

'I was only explaining...'

Teacher, interrupting, 'That's level 2; I'll speak to you at end of the lesson.'

'That's not fair.'

'Don't challenge me. Now you're on level 3, you've lost your lunch time.'

'But I only talked.'

'Still talking. Level 4. I'm calling for your removal. Wait outside.'

Basically, the teacher was engineering the student's removal from the lesson by inconsistent use of the school procedures. In essence this could be said to be an abuse of authority. The student was shown no respect in the dealings with the teacher who, quite frankly, didn't want them in the room.

The problem, of course, was that the teacher-student relationship had been seriously damaged. In fact it was so damaged we ended up having to move the student to another teaching group.

As for the rest of the class, the inconsistency of approach made them resentful. It was their friend who they saw being kicked out, for what they saw as a trivial matter and for what they knew would not have happened to them.

Although less extreme, other forms of inconsistency towards different individuals are when one of the nicest students does something wrong and we let them off. Just because 99.9% of the time these students don a halo doesn't mean they are exempt from the rules that apply to all.

Letting them off causes more resentment, not only towards you for your inconsistency, but towards them for your favoritism.

In this sense, consistent means be fair to all and applying all the rules to all the students in the same way. If you do, all the students will be fair back. Even the naughty ones will respect you.

3) Have high expectations

Always set the bar high and explicitly tell the students what you expect in terms of their behavior, effort and the work they do.

If you are talking to the whole class and there are one or two students not fully paying attention and you let them carry on, then you are implying that you grant permission for others to do the same. If this is not what you want then you need to stop speaking and state, 'My expectations are that if I am speaking to the whole class then I want everyone to pay me full attention. Does everyone understand this? Can you tell me why it's important that you are paying attention?'

Once again, consistency is important here. You have to keep doing this until the behavior you are looking for is embedded. You can't state your high expectation and then let it slip the next time the rule is broken.

This goes for all rules.

Having high expectations and letting the class know you have them also allows you to raise the bar even higher. 'Okay class, I've been very challenging so far and have asked you to do X. You've managed to do this brilliantly, so now we're going to move on to the next level and from now on we are going to do X and Y. I'm sure we'll be able to achieve this in no time at all.'

Notice the positive language I've used here to announce the increase in expectation. I'll discuss this in more detail later.

4)   Keep your promises

Rewards and sanctions are one of the key tools we have to manage behavior in classrooms and enable us to maintain good behavior once we have established it.

One of the most important things we must do with rewards and sanctions is to keep any promises or threats that we make. The consequences for continually not keeping them can seriously undermine you and mean that students' behavior and motivation can be negatively affected.

If you have promised a student that a certificate will be awarded to them at an assembly and it doesn't happen, then that student will feel more let down than if you had never rewarded them in the first place.

Similarly, if you have a misbehaving student in your room and you threaten to call their parents if they repeat the offence and then, once they do repeat it you fail to carry out the threat, you are signaling to the students that you don't follow through with your sanctions. As a result, they will see this as a sign of weakness and begin to misbehave; believing that beyond you telling them to stop in the lesson there will be no escalation in the punishment they get.

In general follow these guidelines to help you:

- don't make promises or threats you know you will not be able to carry out
- make sure any promises and threats are realistic. 'Right, that's it, you are going to be in detention every day for a month.' Really?
- if it's not necessary don't give a specific time scale for your promise or threats: instead of saying, 'I'm going to ring your parents today,' tell them 'Your parents will be informed about this. It might not be today, but they will find out.'
- that said, only make promises and threats that you can achieve relatively quickly – you want your impact to be as immediate impact as possible.

5)   Actually teach good behavior

Children go to school to learn and need to learn how to behave as much as they need to learn the curriculum. What you teach them from a behavioral perspective depends a great deal upon their age and their background.

Young children have much more to learn than older children simply because they are younger and less experienced, but even in groups of the same age there will always be some children whose backgrounds have prepared them to behave better than others.

Whilst the overwhelming majority of parents and carers do a fantastic job in bringing up children to be polite and generally well behaved, they do not have the opportunity to teach their children how to behave in a classroom setting or how to behave for learning. These are a different set of skills that students need to develop.

It's unrealistic, therefore, for us to believe that all children can behave exactly as we want them to without teaching them. Consequently, the onus is on us to ensure they are skilled up. Indeed, it is now very common in schools for students to be taught 'BfL' – Behavior for Learning, to develop those skills.

Behavior for Learning is a subject in itself and I won't go into great detail here except to say that, if it is implemented correctly, it will be part of a whole school initiative which is coordinated by a designated leader and the provision will be planned and structured for all students.

Just as in the same way that you need to follow the school's behavior policy, you should also teach behavior for learning in accordance with any guidelines implemented by any Behavior for Learning policy. You cannot have one teacher saying one thing whilst the rest of the school says something else.

However, it's within your remit as a classroom practitioner that you do teach the students what good behavior is and it is a good idea, should you find it necessary, to take time out from the curriculum and teach a discrete lesson on a particular behavior issue that you wish to address.

Types of things you could teach include:

- why it important to be quiet and listen to the teacher
- how to work in groups
- how to get on with other students in the classroom
- why rules are important
- how to start and end lessons
- how to enter and exit the classroom

There are also other things you may wish to teach them depending on your own teaching style. When I teach I have a 'No Hands Up' rule for when I question the class. Everyone is expected to give an attempt at an answer if I ask them. As many other teachers ask for hands up, I have to teach my class not to put their up for questions.

Another technique I use is that, rather than asking for quiet and waiting for attention, I put my hand in the air. When the children see this, they are to put their hand in the air too and stop talking. This too needs to be taught.

Like all things, you may find that some students learn quicker than others and from time to time you will need to address the Behavior for Learning again – just in the same way you might need to remind students to use punctuation in their writing. From a discipline point of view, once you have taught the behavior you want children to adopt there is less excuse for them to misbehave. There is also much less chance of them not knowing what it is you want when you ask them to behave in a particular way.

6)   Avoid stereotyping and labelling

Young and impressionable minds will cling to anything that gives them self-esteem in front of their peers. If their friends like something they do, they will try to repeat it. If they keep on getting positive feedback from repeating this behavior then we find that that their friends label them. As a response, the label becomes a badge of pride and they then feel almost compelled to live up to expectations.

From here students can quickly adopt social stereotypes: the classroom joker, the bully, the hard-knock, the mouthy back-chatter, the lazy student, the dunce.

Students who engage in negative behaviors in order to boost their self-esteem will find that self-esteem boosted even further if it is reinforced by the teacher. As a result, they will try to continue that behavior in your classroom if you continually give them the feedback they are looking for. In a sense you will be an enabler of their addiction to this type of behavior.

It's very important, therefore that you take steps to prevent this. To do this, you need to remove the psychological rewards they seek from their actions. Telling the class joker that they are funny, referring to them as the 'class joker' or 'funny guy' and joining in at laughing at their pranks are all ways to reaffirm their beliefs and consolidate their status.

Unfortunately, dealing the wrong way with their behavior can have the same effect. If you reprimand them for prankish behavior in an effort to stop it, then you are still telling them what they want. 'I know I'm the class joker because I'm always getting into trouble for it.'

Essentially, the pranks and attempts to be funny are attention seeking behavior and one of the ways to deal with it is to ignore it. Of course, there is a limit to doing this and eventually you will need to reprimand the student.

The best way to do this is to make no reference to the prankish behavior when you talk to the student. Phrases like, 'That's not funny,' just tell the student what they want to hear, especially if it's said in front of others. Instead, refer to their behavior in other terms, such as 'It was inappropriate' or 'You were disrupting my lesson.'

It's worth mentioning here that whilst you try to dismantle any self-esteem gained from being class joker, you need to fill the gap and give them self-esteem from something more positive, in other words, find something else to make them feel good about.

This method applies equally to other stereotypes. Calling a bully 'a bully' will make them feel better rather than worse if they think it will make them look good. Instead discuss the behavior in other ways. I always found using legal terminology with bullies made them wake up and listen. Instead of saying, 'You were bullying,' say, 'You assaulted another student.'

An important factor to remember with all these types of behavior is to separate the behavior from the child. Instead of saying 'You are a bad girl,' we should always refer to the behavior instead, 'that was a bad thing to do.' This then needs to be followed up with a statement that will paint them in a more positive light, 'You're capable of better than that.' Doing this drives a wedge between them and their behavior so that they don't perceive themselves as bad and can go on to adjust their actions in a better way.

7)   Keeping records

I know from personal experience that bureaucracy is the bane of most teachers' working lives and that there is too much paperwork required in today's schools. However, it is important to keep records about a student's behavior. Good schools will have a simple, centralized, computer system that allows you to record incidents of bad behavior in seconds These are essential for tallying up the behavior of problem students as the data can be used as evidence to permanently exclude the worst offending students from school. If that data is lacking it is unlikely that those students could be permanently excluded. That data is also useful evidence for you should you need to contact a child's parents about their behavior.

If you do not have a centralized system, then I would suggest you create your own rewards and behavior tracker using a simple spreadsheet. It's not difficult to do and can save you hours of time trying to remember things should pastoral leaders ask for evidence at a later date.

Many schools also use a whiteboard in lessons so that you can keep a temporary record of misbehavior in a single session. This allows teachers in schools that operate a 'three chance then out' policy to keep a tally of how many chances a student has had before a sanction is given. It also prevents a student arguing that you haven't given a warning as it's on the wall for them to see.

Again, if you are not supplied with one, you can simply create a small grid on an existing whiteboard, have a column for the names of the student and then corresponding columns for each level of warning.

8)   Involving the parents and guardians

Parents and guardians need to be informed about their children's behavior on a regular basis. This includes positives as well as negatives. Most schools do this through regular reports home and through parents' evenings. However, as a classroom teacher it is sometimes helpful to do this when you feel there is the need or desire to do so – and it can have immediate and massive impact on the behavior of individual students.

From a behavior point of view, parents like nothing better to hear that their child is well behaved and a letter or a call home to tell them can help build good relationships between the teacher and the parents. In addition, a child who knows that a teacher will let their parents know how well they are behaving is more likely to behave better for that teacher because they are likely to be rewarded at home for your call. One of the main reasons this happens is that teachers rarely call home to congratulate good behavior, so when it does happen it must mean that their child is especially well behaved.

It's more common that we contact parents over poor behavior, but it essential that we do. Parents need to know if their child is misbehaving so they can support the school in helping that child change their behavior for the better.

Different schools have different procedures for doing this. In my last school contacting parents was done mainly by the pastoral managers – non-teaching staff whose sole responsibility was for the pastoral care of students. These members of staff developed excellent relationships with the parents of even the most challenging students. They were always the ones who contacted home and were the ones parents always contacted when they had a problem. They got to know the children's backgrounds and the out of school issues that were affecting them. If teaching staff had an issue it was the pastoral manager who rang up the parents to inform them.

However, even if this is the type of system you work with, it can always be helpful to speak to a parent yourself. This way you can discuss issues which are affecting your particular lesson or subject and discuss possible ways to deal with behavioral problems.

In the majority of cases, parents are really the big guns when it comes to discipline. You can give students a detention or other form of minimal punishment – parents on the other hand can hand out much tougher love: grounding, taking away the Xbox, banning sweets for younger children or what most teenagers these days consider the ultimate sanction – taking away the phone.

There are, of course, a small but significant number of parents who won't support you. Not only will they not back you up, they will put the blame on you for picking on their child or refuse to let their child do detentions or other sanctions. In these situations it's best to pass the situation on to a senior leader to handle.

Praise and Reward

Praise and reward are two of the best tools you have as a teacher to manage behavior in your classroom and, used effectively, they can eradicate a great deal of bad behavior that you may normally have to face. This section will look at how to use it effectively.

Praise

As educators we need to build up a students' self-esteem. A student who feels good about themselves is more likely to follow rules, work harder and be better motivated to succeed. They are also far more likely to pay attention to those who make them feel good about themselves. So if you are making a student feel good they are going to be more receptive to your advice and guidance and more likely to want to please you by doing well in your lesson.

1) Praise in public

One way to increase a student's self-esteem is to praise them in public. Doing this has three advantages:

- the feel good that you have acknowledged them
- they feel good that their peers know
- they feel pride in that you felt what they did was good enough to let everyone else know.

Praise, however, can have other benefits if it is used correctly, such as:

- using it as a way of getting reticent students to answer and elaborate on answers. 'Brilliant answer, Sophie. Can you make it even better by explaining why?'
- getting a difficult student on your side. 'Excellent entrance into the classroom, Peter, let's see if we can keep that up until the end of the lesson.'
- derailing potential conflict. If Suzie is being challenging today, just when she thinks you are going to reprimand her and give her the excuse she is looking for to 'kick off', give her an easy question and praise her for her wonderful answer. This will disarm her, at least temporarily.
- building relationships. This is an easy one, just praise something personal about the student. 'Cool shoes.' 'Oh, you like [name of pop star]? You have great taste in music.'

The list of things you can say to affect behavior is endless. Here are just a few:

- 'You're sitting very still today, well done.'
- 'That's the quietest you've worked all week, keep it up.'
- 'Excellent listening.'
- 'Good manners!'

- 'You've acted in a very grown up way by tidying up.'
- 'Well done, you've not shouted out once today.'
- 'Thank you for not disrupting, that's very mature behavior.'
- 'Thank you for sharing your pencils, well done.'
- 'Not even a warning today, that's brilliant. Keep it up.'

2)   Praising the few to manage the many

Another use for praise is that you can say it to one person but know that when you do it will have an effect on all the others.

In my last school we had an issue with school ties which the students used to loosen so much that the knots were often nearer their navels than their necks. In order to stop this we began lining students up outside the class and would not let them in the room until the ties had been tightened correctly.

Rather than have to reprimand the students who didn't have their ties done up and create a negative atmosphere before the lesson had started, it was far easier to walk down the line praising all the students who had arrived properly dressed.

As soon as I began praising these students the others all began to follow suit and adjust their ties. The big advantage here is that not only did I manage to get all the students into class without telling them off, I'd also managed to praise every single one of them before they had even entered the room. Double bonus! ↳ *Praise before lesson begins*

This technique can be used continuously throughout all lessons. It massively reduces the friction in the classroom and makes teaching much less stressful. It creates positivity rather than negativity and usually has the desired effect upon achieving desired behavioral outcomes.

So, the next time you ask for quiet and don't get everyone listening, rather than start calling out at individuals or small groups to be quiet, just praise the ones who have already done what you said.

→ publicly
→ praise effort

3)   Praising effort rather than achievement

Unfortunately, many schools are over-focused on achievement and it's all too easy to praise high achievers at the expense of others. However, from a behavior and achievement perspective this is not necessarily the way to make the most substantial gains.

If you constantly publically praise all the students who achieve top marks then the message to the students who don't achieve them is that they are not worthy of praise. To those who know that they are never going to achieve top marks this can be completely demoralizing.

From an achievement perspective this can have dire consequences. A grade D student with the potential to achieve grade C may give up trying and stay at grade D because they only ones who were ever given praise and recognition were the grade A students. In reality, this student may have worked twice as hard to achieve the grade D as the grade A students did to achieve their grade A.

The result for the school is that large numbers of students, particularly those of middle and lower ability will underachieve.

The way to combat this is to praise for effort not for achievement. By all means praise achievement privately, but for public praise focus on the amount of hard work put in. This makes for a level playing field in the classroom and allows everyone the potential to feel recognized and valued. Even the academically weakest student in the class can have their self-esteem built up and be motivated to do well. From a behavioral perspective this will encourage those students to behave better as they are keen to improve and succeed.

4) Other ways to praise

Praise can be given in lots of other ways:

- you can praise students in front of other teachers
- praise students in front of their parents or by calling or writing to their parents
- you can praise on wall displays and in publications like school magazines, websites and newsletters.
- get students to praise each other. If one student has done something praise worthy, get the class to give them a cheer or a round of applause.

There are some exceptions to praising in public and this would be for specific students who may be vulnerable to bullying from others. If you think that praising a student may lead to them being bullied, then it might be better to do it quietly. Use your discretion here.

The great things about praise are that it is free, easy and instantaneous. It won't solve all your problems but it is a fantastic tool that you should be using consistently.

Rewards

In most schools there is usually a whole school rewards system which is administered by senior staff and which rewards students for things like: effort, behavior, achievement, contribution to the school and attendance. Rewards can take any number of forms such as: trips, treats, certificates, money, vouchers, trophies and be handed out to individuals, groups, classes or even larger groups of students.

The principles behind rewarding are often aligned to the school's ethos and its improvement priorities. At one school I worked in, attendance was such an issue that students who had managed to maintain 100% attendance over the course of a year were given significant prizes. One received a bike, another received an iPad. Everyone who had met the minimum attendance level of 95%, several hundred students in total, were taken away on a trip paid for by the school whilst the rest had to stay and do lessons as normal.

The way most systems work in schools is that rewards points are given by staff on a day to day basis and at the end of term these points are totaled up. The ones given rewards are those that have either earned more points than everyone else or those that achieve a threshold level. Some rewards systems specify a target, for example; earn 30 reward points and get a bronze prize, earn 40 and get a silver prize, earn 50 and get a gold prize; while others choose a percentage – the top 50% get to go on a trip. I've worked with both systems and both have their advantages and disadvantages – but both do work if the rewards are given in the correct way.

For the classroom teacher there are clear expectations about rewards which make them different from praise. You can praise anyone, anytime, for any reason to achieve the desired outcome, what you can reward for is prescribed by the school rules and you cannot change this.

Rewarding for behavior

At the end of each half term (around every six weeks) the school leadership team, at one school I worked in, were presented with the rewards data for all students over that time. One thing that struck us as distinctly odd was that many of the students who had received very high rewards for behavior were the same ones who had also received very high numbers of poor behavior points. How could it be that the worst behaved students in the school, the ones that were constantly being removed from lessons, were also the ones who were most highly rewarded for good behavior?

The answer was easily found – there was inconsistency in the teachers' approach to rewarding. A student who was always good would have to do something quite exceptional to get rewarded for their behavior whereas a student who was frequently badly behaved could get rewarded simply for sitting quietly for half an hour. *ensure fair rewards.*

Not only was this unfair on the vast majority of good students it was also a sign of appeasement on behalf of the teachers. They were rewarding these students not because they were well behaved but to keep them well behaved. Rather than rewarding them after a good lesson, they were being offered to the student at the beginning of the lesson as a potential payment for keeping them good. The students were happy because for them it meant going on a trip – in reality it meant going on a trip at the expense of another better deserving student.

The problem was this: whilst you can praise badly behaved students as much as you want to encourage and manage their behavior, you cannot reward them unless they have met the criteria laid down in the school's reward policy. The behavior policy at this school was that all students were expected to comply with school rules, follow all reasonable staff instructions and meet the basic expectations for behavior. What was happening was that teachers were rewarding poorly behaved students for following the behavior policy (a basic expectation for all students), not for meeting the criteria for rewards.

To be rewarded, behavior had to be exemplary: students needed to be especially helpful, highly co-operative, be a role model, volunteer to go first, take responsibility for something etc., on top of behaving as expected throughout the lesson. Rewarding for anything less than this was lowering the high expectations the school had set for its behavior.

The issue for the leadership team was that some staff had begun to use rewards as a behavior management tool. It was their way of keeping control in their rooms. What they didn't realize was the impact in had in other lessons and across the school as a whole. It caused many well behaved students to feel aggrieved at the situation, especially on trip days when they walked into school to see the badly behaved students waving goodbye to them from the back seat of the bus.

What should have happened is that in the lesson, the teacher should have praised the badly behaved students in the following way: 'You've done really well today. Thank you. I'd like to give you a reward point next lesson, but to do that you'll also need to ….' This way you are challenging them to the next level of behavior which might have genuinely met the criteria for a reward.

In conclusion, therefore:

- don't reward for what is expected of every student
- reward only against the criteria
- reward for above and beyond
- reward for effort and contribution
- be consistent – treat all students the same
- don't have favorites

Using Positive Language

When you discuss behavior then at some point you will have to think about psychology; for this book, this section on language use is where I will address it the most.

I'm not going to discuss psychological theory here because that is not the purpose of this book, but in essence, educational psychologists believe that if we use language in a positive rather than a negative way when we speak to students then we are far more likely to achieve the behavioral outcomes we are looking for.

Students are more receptive to positivity; they are more likely to accept what you are saying as you are not creating psychological barriers; it is perceived as less threatening so students do not automatically set themselves up in opposition to you; and the way you speak offers them a solution rather than a problem.

1)   What is positive language?

Using positive language basically means that instead of using words with negative connotations we use words with positive ones. Rather than telling children what we don't want them to do, we tell them what we do want them to do.

Here are some examples:

- 'Will you be quiet?' becomes, 'Please listen carefully.'
- 'Don't shout out,' becomes, 'Please put your hand up.'
- 'Stop messing around,' becomes, 'Get on with your work please?'
- 'Stop interrupting,' becomes, 'Wait your turn to speak, please.'

For those who think that using positive language weakens the teachers' authority, a closer analysis of the language shows this not to be the case. All the positive sentences used above are imperatives (commands) and are assertive with regard to the outcomes they wish to achieve. What makes them stronger is that they explicitly state the outcome they wish to achieve, whereas the negative alternative only implies the outcome. 'Stop messing around' doesn't actually mean 'get on with your work.'

In addition, the use of good manners with a positive instruction shows politeness, respect for the student and models good behavior. In contrast, the use of good manners in conjunction with a negative comment sounds incongruous. To say, 'Please stop messing around,' suggests desperation, vulnerability and lack of authority.

To really make the use of manners a powerful tool, replace 'please' with 'thank you.' 'Please' is used with a request to do something – a cousin of the word 'plead.' 'Thank you,' is said after something has been done as requested. Using 'thank you' before something has been done implies an expectation that it will be done. In this way it reinforces the explicit command that you have issued but making it polite at the same time. So, next time instead of saying, 'Get on with your work, please,' say, 'Get on with your work, thank you.'

Using positive language can be applied to a whole range of situations including the marking of students' work. Where once we would have written, 'This is untidy! Do it again!!!' A more positive comment would be, 'Rewrite this piece of work in a neater way, thank you.'

Of course there may be moments of urgency when positivity isn't the most important factor. Whilst, 'I want you to go home in one piece today,' may be the positive way to say it, I'm sure that in an emergency situation, shouting out, 'Don't put your fingers near the electric saw!' would probably have a more instantaneous effect.

For me, changing the way I spoke to the students was the hardest thing to achieve simply because my normal way of speaking seemed to be hard-wired. When speaking a foreign language, which is not my forte at all, I usually say it in English first before translating: and this is how I managed to begin to move from negative to positive speaking in lessons.

2) Choices and Consequences

Another important way to have a positive effect on behavior is to offer students choices about their actions. By doing this, you are making the student fully responsible for their choice of action and making it clear to them what the consequences of their behavioral choices will be. For example:

'Okay John, you are now on level two for your behavior. You now have a choice. You can choose to stop misbehaving, in which case no further action will be taken, or you can choose to carry on misbehaving. If you choose to carry on, the consequence will be a detention. What are you going to choose?'

The last question, 'What are you going to choose?' is an important closing sentence as it requires the student to openly state their choice to you, which works as a form of promise to behave better. If they then continue to misbehave you need to explain what will happen using the terms 'choice' and 'consequence.'

'Unfortunately you have made the choice to continue misbehaving and the consequences of that, which you were already aware of, will be a detention.'

This works because in the end the child begins to realize that it is not you who have put them in detention, that decision was theirs – they made the choice.

This is a very popular way to deal with behavior in schools. I have worked in schools who have actually named their behavioral system after these words – one school called it 'Consequences' and another 'Choices' – words that all the children in the school were fully familiar with. In both schools, these strategies were very successful.

Everyday Techniques

So far I have discussed some of the major things you need to implement and some of the principles you need to adhere to in order to build a well-managed classroom. In this next section I will cover some of the everyday tips and techniques you can use which will complement the things mentioned so far.

1) Meet and greet

A simple but effective way to get a lesson off to a good start is to meet the students as they arrive. Whether you line them up before they enter or let them straight in it gives you the opportunity to personally greet every one of them before the lesson begins. Doing this:

- establishes your authority over the teaching space because you are acting as a gatekeeper; you can delay entry to anyone who hasn't turned up with the correct attitude to learn
- allows you to personally interact with students enabling you to maintain good relationships with them
- lets you sort out any issues before they enter the room such as uniform problems or students with phones
- gives you the chance to hold back any student who needs a reminder of something before the lesson begins
- lets you rearrange seating

2) Bury the hatchet and clean the slate

It's always important to remember that there is a difference between the person and the behavior. Whilst we cannot be tolerant of a student's poor behavior we do have to give the student a chance to prove themselves the next time we see them.

For this reason, no matter how badly behaved they were in the previous lesson, we have to start a new lesson from scratch. We cannot hold grudges or continue from where the last incident left off. That does not mean we cannot remind them of their previous bad behavior and warn them about the coming lesson, but it needs to be done in the right manner. 'Okay, Stephen, you didn't show the best of your behavior last lesson. I'm looking forward to seeing a big improvement today. Do you think you can do that?'

There are several reasons for beginning each lesson afresh:

- it rebuilds the relationship between you and the student
- it gives the student the opportunity to prove themselves
- it prevents the student being put into an anxious state of mind, worrying about how you will treat them after their previous behavior
- it helps prevent the student from playing truant from your lesson

3)   Use students' first names when you talk to them

Something as simple as using students' names when you talk to them has a positive effect upon their reactions to you. It shows them you know who they are, it reinforces your relationship with them and it's a sign of respect that they value.

When you do this in the classroom it works as a behavior management technique because the respect shown by you has a way of pacifying poor behavior. Using first names establishes a behavioral precedent for the lesson that makes it much more difficult for the student to break.

If the student does need reprimanding, then using their first name when you talk to them makes them more receptive to what you have to say and more difficult for them to challenge you, the result being that you're much more likely to have things go your way.

How do you remember names? Print out photographs from the schools database or if the students are always based in the same classroom have a picture wall.

4)   Getting lessons off to a good start

By its nature, the start of a lesson is often the most chaotic part and a lesson that begins badly can often snowball out of control. It's always better if you establish a clear routine for the beginning of a lesson so that your students quickly get to know what to expect as soon as they enter the room.

Common issues with the starts of lessons can be:

- children arriving at different times
- personal issues to deal with as they arrive (one has a nosebleed, two others have fallen out and are arguing and a fourth has lost their money out of their pocket)
- some students are keen to have a personal conversation with you as they enter the room
- books need handing out
- the desks and chairs need rearranging from the last lesson and you haven't had time to move them
- the register has to be taken
- several students took their books home and forgot to bring them in for the lesson
- half a dozen students haven't got a pen
- there's a chair missing

And if you are an unorganized teacher then of course there are your own problems on top of these: in which folder did you save the file with today's lesson plan? What did you call that PowerPoint? I know the worksheets are in here somewhere! 'What do you mean we did that last lesson?'

All of these can contribute to a 'sloppy start' and whilst your attention is diverted to sorting out the issues, the students are left to their own devices; the noise gets louder, misbehavior begins and nothing gets learned. A lesson that starts at 9.00am can go 15 minutes before order is established and work begins. This of course is unacceptable. So here are some tips for making sure as little of this affects you as possible:

- always make sure that the class that leaves is the one to rearrange desks for the next lesson
- have a short piece of preparatory work ready for the children to do as soon as they enter the lesson with instructions clearly set out
- have plenty of pens, pencils, rulers and other essentials readily available for all students who do not have their own
- have spare paper readily available for all students who forget books
- be firm with students who are trying to distract you from starting. 'Not now, I have things I need to do. I'll deal with it later.'

Once you have got the above put in place, you then have several minutes, whilst the students are completing the preparatory work, to hand out the books; take a register; send someone for a missing chair; direct the nosebleed to first aid, arbitrate the falling out; and sort out the lost money. By the time the late comers arrive you will be finishing the preparatory task and ready to begin the lesson proper, so they will miss out on very little.

The key difference, from a behavioral point of view, is to get the students on task first and then deal with issues. Just make sure you have everything they need (a task, pen, paper, etc.) to get them settled quickly.

The impact of setting a task for students to do as soon as they entered the lesson can be enormous. It was so successful in trials at one of the schools I worked in that we decided to make it compulsory in all lessons. It's settling effect set the tone for the entire lesson and had a real impact on reducing the numbers of students getting sanctioned for poor behavior,

The task doesn't have to be too demanding; indeed it could be something as simple as recapping the last lesson, matching up key words to their definitions, even a word search. What it does do is establish a routine that work begins as soon as students enter the room – they don't have to wait for everyone to be there or for books to be handed out; they don't even need the teacher to instruct them. The routine settles them down quickly and gives the teacher space to sort out problems. Completing the preparatory work then allows the second phase of the lesson to start smoothly.

5)   Give instructions one at a time

This is an easy technique to use that allows you to communicate more clearly, get things done with less complication, gives students the chance to follow instructions without getting confused and generally makes for a smoother, better behaved beginning to a task or lesson.

Does the following instruction sound familiar? 'Okay class, open your books, write today's date, copy the title from the board and then do exercise 23 on page 56 of your text books. Remember to underline your title and write out the questions before you write the answer.'

In reality, there are six instructions here, not one. If this is how you normally communicate instructions, think of how its complexity impacts upon the behavior in your lesson. Whilst some students will have listened well and taken on board all you have said, others will have partially taken it all in; another group will have lost the thread by the time the second instruction was given; and a final group will think they understand but will have got the instructions totally wrong.

As a result, you'll get the following reactions: some of the students will begin working; some of the ones who could begin working are having to explain your instructions to some of those who haven't; even worse, some of those who think they know but have got it wrong will be telling others how to get it wrong too. The rest will either be sat there looking confused or have their hand in the air looking at you for clarification.

The result is twofold. Firstly, the teacher has a rise in stress levels because they can't understand why their students can't follow such a simple instruction and begin to lose their temper with those who haven't started yet or who haven't understood. Secondly, the students who are confused are off task and begin to disrupt those who do seem to know. They then get resentful at being scolded by the teacher and feel belittled at not being able to follow a seemingly simple instruction.

In the end, the teacher will need to go through the instructions again and a less happy class will start the work late. Learning time will be lost, relationships damaged.

Instead it's much easier to do the following:

'Open you books, please.' (Pause and check.)

'Now write the date.' (Pause and check.)

'Copy and underline the title from the board.' (Pause and check.)

'Everyone finished? Good, now turn to page 56 of your exercise books.' (Pause and check.)

'Can you find exercise 23?' (Pause and check.)

'I want you to do exercise 23. Remember to write the questions before answering. Does everyone understand? Okay, begin.'

Generally, the younger the students, the better it is to adopt this method. However, it is also a method that you should do with students with Asperger's and autism and is also beneficial to students with other learning and behavioral difficulties.

You will find it makes thing flow much better and calms the mood in the classroom. The time lost through slowing things down is gained because no one has to wait for clarification.

6)   Reprimand in private

There's a commonly used acrostic used in many schools called 'PIPRIP' which stands for Praise In Public, Reprimand In Private. I've already discussed the virtues of praising in public in the Praise section of this book so this section will concentrate on reprimanding in private.

Before I discuss the benefits of reprimanding in private, I will begin with the caveat that doing it is not always practical and sometimes it's not always called for; you need to use your professional judgment. If you are in the middle of explaining something to the class then taking a child to one side right there and then can cause more problems than it's worth. Similarly, taking them outside for a trivial offence may seem a little extreme.

In these situations a quiet reminder may have to suffice. You can also use facial expressions, gesture and eye contact, which I discuss in the next section, to reprimand them unobtrusively.

There are, however, situations where reprimanding in private is called for, these are:

- when the student has committed a serious misdemeanor
- when there may be the risk of confrontation
- where other students may try to get involved
- when the discussion will disrupt the lesson
- when it will help diffuse a conflict between students

In these situations it is always advisable to ask the student to speak to you outside the room. Do this calmly. Saying, 'Can I have a word?' is a much better approach than shouting, 'Get out!' and stomping angrily to the door. When done calmly it doesn't get the student angry and anxious so reduces the risk of confrontation.

The main advantage of speaking to them outside of the room is that they are less likely to feel belittled or embarrassed in front of their peers. A student who feels belittled is going to react in a way that makes them look better in front of their friends and the way they do this is to speak back, challenge and argue with you – leading to the chance of a flashpoint, especially as there is no way you can let a child undermine your authority in front of the class.

Removing the student from their peers immediately takes away this problem and means that you can have a discussion where the child's focus is on you and not on their friends. It means there is a greater chance of success as you can ask for and give explanations and then ask for guarantees before re-entering the room.

I always give the following tips about these conversations:

- make it clear that it is their choice about how they behave and if they choose to continue to misbehave they will be bringing further sanctions upon themselves
- ask for a guarantee from the student that their behavior will improve
- ask if the student is happy that the issue is now resolved
- make the student promise not to disrupt the lesson by talking about the conversation when they go back to class
- as you both re-enter the room, say 'Thank You,' to the student out loudly for the class to hear – this will stop the class being too interested in what has happened.

The one other thing you need to remember is that it isn't really acceptable to leave a classroom of students unattended. If one of them comes to harm whilst you are out of the room then you are culpable. So, if you don't have another adult in the room, what I always do is stand in the doorway and have the student out of sight of the rest of the class. If there is a window in the door, and there is in most classrooms these days, then I might slightly close the door behind me and keep one eye on the class through the window. I then talk in a low voice so as not to disturb the lesson or let them know what I'm talking about. This also works for keeping the discussion calm. If you talk quietly and calmly, the child will talk back quietly and calmly too.

7) Using gesture, facial expressions and eye contact

It's always best to keep any behavioral intervention to its absolute minimum. The less intrusive you can be with the class as a whole, the better. Indeed, many experienced teachers can deal with one student's misbehavior without the rest of the class even knowing and the way most of them do this is through using hand gestures, facial expressions and eye contact.

The most important of the above is eye contact because until you have this, you don't have the student's full attention. I used to work with one teacher who was an absolute genius at controlling students with just his eyes. He'd silently just look at a student until they had noticed him and then keep looking. At first they'd look away to avoid his gaze then look back to see if he'd stopped. Realizing that he hadn't, they would then give him the eye contact he was demanding. They soon understood that what they had done was not acceptable and that they needed to get back on with their work. Once the student was back on task, he'd stop and get on with something else.

These actions did not interrupt the class and usually lasted only a few seconds – but they were highly effective.

Of course, this was not something that the teacher had developed over night. One significant aspect of its ability to work was that the teacher was a well-established member of staff and that throughout school, children referred to these acts as 'The Stare'. Even children who had never been taught by him had heard of this and thus, if he stared at you, it had a meaning that the whole school knew.

Whilst being able to simply look at a child with a blank face and get what you want might take a while to do, the rest of us can combine eye contact with easily readable facial expressions and hand gestures that can signal our intentions to students in an unobtrusive manner. These can include:

- raising your eyebrows to warn
- putting a finger to your lips to quieten

- wagging a finger or shaking your head to say no
- showing the flat palm of your hand to signal stop
- Putting finger to forehead to mean 'think'
- Frowning to show disapproval

As a consequence of being unobtrusive, the student at the receiving end is much less likely to respond in an obtrusive way because you have not publically scolded them; their ego and self-esteem are still intact so they have little reason to make a fuss about it.

8)   Don't be the biggest disruptor

A few years ago I attended a training session on behavior management by a famous educationalist. Part of the session involved the expert showing videos of himself working in the classroom with students he had never met before so we could see his best practice in action.

Whilst there were some rather good points to take home at the end of the day, one thing did strike me: he never stopped talking. The expert was a huge supporter of praising students and once he'd set the class a task he then proceeded around the classroom loudly praising every single student.

Now, whilst I'm a huge supporter of praising in public, I also think that if you set a task in which you require the students to work independently without interrupting each other, then you need to make sure that you do the same. By all means work quietly with students who need help and visit as many students to look at their work as you can – but don't disrupt the class yourself. You need to save things for the right time otherwise your disruption will have the same negative impact on behavior and progress as student disruption.

There are several other ways teachers can disrupt their own lessons, these include:

- being unorganized and having to stop an activity half way through to explain something you forgot.
- letting students get you into a conversation about something not related to the lesson and then telling the whole class about it. Children love to hear personal stories and anecdotes from teachers and there can be a place for it in lessons – but make sure it's in the right place and the right time.
- having conversations with other members of staff. Teachers often enter other teachers' lessons for a variety of reasons and this can sometimes lead to them having a conversation which will distract others. They really shouldn't come in at all unless it's absolutely

necessary and only then if they do it with as little fuss as possible. Try not to do it to others yourself.

- setting a task, letting the students begin and then start playing around with what's on the white board. If you get the students working and then begin googling things or putting up presentations on the white board for the next section of the lesson then the children are going to stop and focus on the board too. Eventually, some will begin talking about it and even talking to you about it. 'Is that video for us?' 'Why are you googling that?' The simple solution, have a dual screen or turn the whiteboard off until it is needed.

9)   Deal with issues later – lessons are for learning only

I find that, particularly with younger students, there are a great number of personal issues that need dealing with. With elementary school students in particular there seems to be a constant barrage of children who have fallen out over trivial things. They often begin to argue in class and if you don't spot it yourself one of them will feel the need to stop you in mid flow to tell you about it. These trivial things can include: arguing over a pencil, not sharing a book, someone has been looking at their work and a hundred other little things that older children would either not worry about or just sort out for themselves.

That said, in older children, whilst the number of incidents of falling out are much less frequent, when they do arise they are usually of a greater magnitude.

Whatever the issue, the impact hinders progress and needs to be resolved. One of the best ways to do this is to make it quite clear that you will help them resolve the issue in their own time but not in lesson time.

Once you have said this, split the warring factions up for the rest of the lesson and then summon them back either at a break or lunch time. Make sure that you go through the matter in a thorough way by giving both students opportunity to speak without interruption, respond to each other and discuss a solution.

Not only should you try to genuinely resolve the matter, but you also need to point out that it's not worth their while falling out over trivial matters as it will result in them losing lots of their own time trying to resolve the problem.

Once you have done this with a few of the class, the rest will soon get the message and so, after a short while of teaching them, all you will have to say is, 'If you fall out, we'll discuss it over lunchtime. Do you want to waste your lunchtime or are you going to stop it now and get on?' They'll choose to stop.

Sometimes, however, you may need to be a little more flexible with how you deal with these issues. I was once forced into the position of having to recast a production for a drama exam, for 18 year old students, because a severe fall out resulted in the entire class splitting itself into two opposing camps. In order to get the learning going again, I took the practical option and rearranged working groups.

10)   Know the child before making assumptions about behavior

If there's one mistake teachers make which makes us feel guilty it's reprimanding a student for a misdemeanor when there are genuine extenuating circumstances. You wouldn't contemplate giving a child a detention for not doing their homework the previous evening if, for example, their grandmother had just passed away. However, many of us unwittingly commit these errors because we take things for granted and make assumptions about a child's behavior before issuing a sanction.

For this reason, we should always seek to find out why a student has done something wrong before acting on what we perceive. 'Can you explain why you didn't do your homework? Was there a reason why you were talking when I was explaining something?'

Asking these questions not only prevents you making a fool of yourself, but it also gives the students the impression that you are fair, show concern for them and are prepared to make an exception when situations genuinely warrant it. It shows you to have a human side which your students will respect you for and in response you will find them repaying you with better behavior.

11)   Effective lesson endings

If you work with the same class all day, bringing one lesson calmly to an end works wonders in getting the next lesson off to a good start. If you work with a range of different classes, then how you end your lesson will directly affect the beginning of the next teacher's class. If they are all hyped up and over excited, that teacher is going to have a difficult time settling those children down to work.

Ending a class well means, that after completing the work, the room is left tidy, books and other resources are packed away and the children are quietly and calmly dismissed.

There are various techniques that can be used here; one I particularly like is the table competition. You give a small reward, each lesson, to the first table that can tidy up, pack away and get themselves quiet in readiness for leaving or for the next session. For me, the reward is usually that they are the first to be allowed to leave.

Another technique is to ask for a minute of silence before the lesson ends, during which they are to hand in books and tidy their desks.

When dismissing the class, do it in stages so there is not a rush for the door. Stand by the door so you can supervise their exit and say goodbye individually.

Using Your Voice

The voice is by far one of the most important tools in a teacher's tool box. We use it as the primary means for explaining, questioning, instructing and informing our students and without it, we wouldn't really be able to teach. However, it's also a key component in managing the behavior of students, not only in what we say but also in how we say it.

Human minds are very astute at understanding that the way we say something can show our feelings and communicate our intentions. Here are some general tips on how to use your voice to get the behavior you want in your class.

1)   Don't shout at the whole class

Shouting at the whole class can have very negative effects. It sends out a message that not only that you are angry, but that you are angry with everyone. This will breed resentment in those who have done nothing wrong. Secondly, the anger shown will make students feel uneasy and create a bad atmosphere in the room.

We tend to shout at a whole class in two types of circumstance, firstly because if the students are very noisy it's an easy way to get everyone's attention and secondly we use it to convey disappointment on those rare occasions where a lot of people in the class have done something wrong or failed to live up to expectation.

With the former, it's much better to use another kind of signal to get everyone to stop what they are doing and listen. A much preferred technique, used by many, is simply to raise one hand in the air and keep it there. When a student sees you do this, they are required to do the same and anyone who sees another student doing this are required to follow suit. Eventually, within a few seconds, everyone will be sitting silently with their hands in the air. This is a quiet and unaggressive way to bring the class to order and works well, provided you embed it successfully and use it consistently.

With the latter, it should always be remembered that, even when there is a lot of misbehavior, not every single child in the room will have been badly behaved. It is simply unfair to shout at the innocent students.

Shouting also gives the impression that you are losing control of your temper. A calm, authoritative and assertive approach is much better.

2) Don't shout at individuals

It can be very tempting at times to give a badly misbehaving student a real dressing down in front of the class. I've seen countless students being bawled at by irate teachers over the years. There's always that one student who will just keep going over the line again and again and eventually the teacher gets to the point that they let rip.

However, it's not good idea to do this. As discussed earlier, it belittles students, damages relationships, destroys lessons and if you are genuinely angry it can potentially lead to a flashpoint situation.

Take them outside and deal with it away from the rest of the class.

3) Talk quietly to gain attention

Teacher trainers always say that your voice should be loud and clear so that the whole class can hear. Whilst this is true, talking quietly can be a good little trick to bring down the noise level in the classroom and get greater attention.

Sometimes, when you speak, there maybe people not paying full attention, perhaps they are fiddling with pens or whispering. Many of them can get away with this because the volume of your own speaking acts as a cover – no one can hear the pens rattling or the whispering when you are speaking loudly. By quieting down, they have to be even quieter to listen and little noises in the background soon begin to get noticed. Once noticed, they usually stop.

Once you have got the attention you need, you can then begin to talk a little louder.

4) Talking slowly in the classroom

I'm not suggesting here that we talk so slowly that we begin to drone and put everyone to sleep, but instead, we need to remember that students need time to assimilate all the things we tell them. In a similar way to the need to give instruction one at a time, we need to speak slowly enough that everything we say is said clearly and understood.

Rattling off words like bullets from a machine gun will mean that much of what we say is not heard clearly or is misinterpreted, leading to problems later on when students have done the wrong thing or are constantly asking for things to be reiterated. Save time and prevent future problems by saying it slowly and clearly.

It should be noted here that we tend to speak at our quickest when we feel most under pressure – it is no doubt at these times when we should be most focused on slowing down the pace of how we speak.

5)   Using the correct tone of voice

Whilst shouting is generally associated with volume, it is often combined with an angry tone of voice – and it's often the tone of voice that is more damaging than the volume.

In order to control behavior we need to use a wider range of vocal skills to get the responses we want and in particular we need to have a repertoire of tones, or moods, of voice.

These include:

- firm and assertive: for dealing with issues
- polite but authoritative: when issuing directions or instructions
- excited and interested: when motivating and enthusing about subject content
- caring and empathetic: when dealing with a student's problems
- jolly: when something fun is happening or making students feel happy
- congratulatory: for rewarding and praising

Try to avoid:

- condescension and patronization
- sarcasm
- indifference
- bitterness
- anger
- sounding bored or miserable

Good Lessons Lead to Good Behavior

It's becoming increasingly common for school leaders to lay the blame for poor behavior on teachers for delivering lessons that do not engage the interests or cater for the abilities of all the students in the class.

Poor behavior, of course, can be caused by a whole range of things, ineffective behavior management being perhaps the major cause. However, school leaders are right; if children are bored or the work given to them is too easy or too hard they switch off and begin to misbehave.

Student surveys, which are routinely undertaken by many schools, usually highlight teachers or subjects which the students find boring. School leaders triangulate this information with the results from lesson observations and data on behavior and the conclusions are obvious: teachers who deliver lessons the students find uninteresting, too easy or too hard have a higher level of student discipline problems.

The solution to this is straightforward; teachers can reduce the potential for poor behavior if they differentiate work for all abilities, have a variety of activities in lessons and enable students to learn through a variety of VAK (visual, auditory and kinesthetic) learning styles. The next section of this book will deal with these three areas.

1)   Differentiation

Differentiation, setting work of appropriate challenge for students of all abilities, is a key requirement of contemporary teaching and should be part of every lesson in order to make sure that all students are given the opportunity for making progress. However, many teachers either don't do it, do it too infrequently or don't do it correctly.

If we don't differentiate not only is progress hindered but behavior can be affected also. If you pitch the work solely at the middle ability students in your group then the higher ability students will finish quickly and find themselves bored by the lack of challenge and the lower ability students will find the work too challenging and will switch off, becoming demoralized and disinterested.

Once a child is bored they will begin to disrupt the ones that are working and soon the whole class can fall into disarray.

Using data to differentiate correctly

To differentiate correctly you need to analyze the data you have available for the students in your class. At what level are they working? What are their targets? Do they have any special needs?

Once you know these facts you can then arrange your class into three broad bands: lower, middle and higher ability. Do this for all your classes. Even if you have been given a class of higher or lower ability students, within that group you will have some that find the work easier or harder than others.

Once you have done this, you can then go about setting appropriate work for each ability group during lessons.

The three types of differentiation

In the contemporary classroom, there are three different ways in which a teacher can differentiate the work for different abilities, these are: differentiation by content, process and product.

1) Differentiation by content

Using this method means that you vary the content of your lesson for each ability group. If, for example, you were exploring a scene from Shakespeare, the lower ability group might be given a modern transcription, the middle ability group might be given the original text with margin notes, whilst the higher ability group could just be given the original text without the notes.

In a history lesson looking at the presidency of JF Kennedy, the lower ability group might look at biographies of Kennedy's life, the middle ability might be looking at the changes taking place within American society at the time and the higher group might be looking at how the American political landscape affected Kennedy's decision making and the consequences that followed.

In a math lesson covering equations, a teacher may provide graded worksheets, each of differing level of challenge. Students can start at a level suitable to them and then progress upwards as they complete each worksheet.

Differentiation by content, therefore, means providing different resources for students of different ability to work on. It can also mean they may be working on different aspects of a theme or topic than other members of the class.

Differentiation by process

Process refers to the activities children undertake to learn. So, for example, in a science lesson for elementary students which looks at how plants grow, the lower ability students might play an interactive game where they water a plant and put it out in the sunshine; the middle ability group could watch a video about how water and light affect plant growth; and the higher ability students might experiment with feeding plants differing amounts of water, putting them in differently lit places and subjecting them to different temperatures.

In a class about bullying, the lower ability students could create a survey about bullying, the middle ability groups could interview people about bullying and the higher ability group could create a role-play about the effects of bullying.

In these examples, the content is still the same, but the process by which each group learns is different.

③ Differentiation by product

The product is the final result of the learning – the finished piece of work. In a group studying a class reader, for example, there may be some children who can write well and others who can barely write at all. In this situation you could have the final piece of work of the lower ability students to be a recorded video of them answering questions about the text. The middle ability group could produce PowerPoint presentation with images and some text whilst the higher ability group could be asked to produce an extended piece of writing.

In a math lesson about 3d shapes, the lower ability group could be asked to create 3D shapes using modelling equipment, the middle ability group could be asked to provide a wall display of different shapes labelled with their attributes and the higher ability group could be asked to write down how they would teach other students about 3d shapes and their attributes.

Again, whilst students are still studying the same theme or topic, the final product that they are aiming to complete is differentiated according to their ability.

It's not necessary to differentiate by content, process and product at the same time and nor is it expected that every single activity in a lesson will be differentiated. However, by setting work appropriate to the abilities of each student you make the work both challenging and accessible. In this way they are much more likely to engage in the work set and maintain good behavior.

2)   Variety of activities

Keeping children focused is essential for good behavior and providing a variety of activities can be the key to successfully doing this.

There are quite a few theories which discuss how long people can maintain concentration for and what the maximum length of time we should spend on a single activity should be. Over recent years these have become influential in education and have led to the popularity of lessons which are made up of a series of shorter tasks rather than having one long task which takes up the whole lesson.

Having worked in a classroom for over 20 years I can agree that some children can concentrate better than others and that concentration levels can vary depending on a student's personal interest in the subject, their motivation and a whole range of other factors. However, the '25 minute maximum' rule that many people adhere to is not applicable to all students at all times. Some students can breeze through 25 minutes and will complain it's too short, whilst to others it feels like a lifetime. Getting the timing of activities right, therefore, will require you to know your class well and also require you to use your judgment in a lesson. If you have planned for an activity to last 15 minutes and all the class are fully engaged and enjoying it, let it carry on a bit longer. If they are losing interest earlier, then put an end to it and move on.

We do, however, have a duty to develop students' concentration spans: not only do we have to prepare them for coping with lengthy examinations, we also have to prepare them for the demands of the working world. When they grow up and get jobs we don't want our future surgeons and airline pilots to start losing focus half an hour into an operation or a transatlantic flight.

However, it is still very important that within lessons we try to vary activities. Children may need to develop the ability to concentrate for longer, but that needs to be done over time. Varying activities can keep children interested, make learning more fun and engaging and prevent boredom from negatively affecting classroom behavior.

Generally speaking, the younger the children the more you need to vary the activities going on. As they mature and their concentration skills develop we can lengthen the activities and do less of them.

If we link this with differentiation, it might be that one way to differentiate within a class is to give less able students more activities with short duration whist the more able are given fewer activities with longer duration.

Mixing things up to vary what goes on in a lesson can be very easy to do. If you have an hour's lesson you can build in time for any of the things below:

Grouping variations:

- Independent work
- Paired work
- Small group work
- Whole class work or questions

Activity Variations

- Reading
- Writing
- Practical activities
- Discussion / debate
- Watching / listening to video or presentations
- Research
- IT activities
- Questioning, feedback and plenary sessions

There are unlimited things you can do under these headings, but here's just one example of the variety that could be achieved in a single hour:

- 5 minute paired prep work on arrival
- 2 minute questions on the prep work
- 10 minute introductory presentation
- 20 minute practical work in small groups based on the introduction
- 3 minute question and answer session on the work done to check progress
- 10 minutes independent written work evaluating the practical work done
- 5 minutes to prepare discussion of the evaluations
- 10 minutes plenary – whole class debate on the findings of the practical work.
- 5 minutes spare – to set up / pack away / hand out homework or extend any other activity where needed.

The example above has 8 different activities, none of which last longer than 20 minutes. It gives a student the opportunity to work independently, in a pair, in a small group and participate in a whole class debate; and the activities include writing, watching / listening to a presentation, discussion, answering questions and practical work.

This range will help ensure that boredom does not set in and knowing that there will be a range of activities helps the student cope because they know that no single activity will go on for too long. As a result, behavioral issues arising from lack of concentration and boredom can be dramatically reduced.

3) VAK – visual, auditory and kinesthetic learning styles

The knowledge about VAK learning styles has been around for a long time and many teachers will have attended some course or had some training on it. My experience, however, is that too few teachers give it much consideration and that only in schools where the leadership team endeavor to embed it, is it really taken seriously.

In short, the theory is that all of us have a preferred learning style which is sort of hard wired into our brains. Some of us prefer to watch things, some prefer to listen, others prefer to do things; and because we prefer these things, we learn better if we do them this way.

My take on this is that whilst it is helpful to let a child learn using their preferred learning style, doing so all the time might prevent them from developing their brains in other ways. If all we do for a visual learner is let them watch things, then we are not going to develop their ability to learn from listening or doing. If a few years down the line they find themselves in a university lecture theatre and are unable to take anything on board, we will have done them a disservice.

For behavioral reasons, however, knowing a child's VAK preference can help us to find activities which will keep them engaged and interested. It will help make lessons more fun and reduce problems that come from boredom. VAK preferences, therefore, can become another element of the teacher's way of differentiating work for the class.

Here are a few examples of how this can be achieved:

Learning about a scene from Shakespeare:

- visual learners read the text out loud
- auditory learners can listen to them and ask questions
- kinesthetic learners can act out what they hear

Learning how to subtract 9 from a two digit number:

- visual learners work it out using a number line
- auditory learners work in pairs explaining and listening to each other work out how to solve the problems
- kinesthetic learners work with an abacus or counters

From a practical point of view, doing this every lesson might be difficult to achieve; however, if you are differentiating by content, process and product and varying the activities in a lesson, then it becomes part of the mix of ingredients that can make lessons far more enjoyable and consequently improve behavior.

Adding these elements to your lessons can change students' attitude to your classes overnight – if they are looking forward to being there you've sorted out the behavior before they've even entered the room.

Higher Level Behavior

The previous sections all dealt with the basics of getting students to behave well in class and how to deal with incidents of misbehavior. Current pedagogical practice, however, requires good behavior to be more than mere compliance with school rules. What school leaders look for today are students whose behavior actually contributes to the learning taking place. This requires students to be:

- skilled in cooperative learning
- responsible for their own and others' learning
- resilient in the face of challenge
- able to work independently

This section will look at techniques that will move behavior beyond mere compliance and up to the levels of engagement and interaction that modern schools require to raise the levels of progress even higher.

1)   Cooperative Strategies

If higher level behavior requires students to help each other to learn, then the task of the teacher is to be able to get them to cooperate to solve problems.

To enable students to develop the skills to do this, the best thing you could do is to incorporate cooperative strategies into your everyday teaching.

Co-operative strategies are a progressive form of group work that require all students to participate in the activities and, through doing so, develop their skills in sharing, turn-taking, interacting and cooperating.

The problem with old fashioned group work is that it's an ideal opportunity for some students to sit back and let everyone else do the work. These students don't learn, don't help others learn and are off task, distracting their peers. They are often one of the primary reasons why quite a lot of teachers are put off doing group work and find it very hard work on the occasions when they do.

Cooperative strategies on the other hand prevent students taking time out because they are structured in such a way that all students have to take part. Take a basic strategy like 'Think, Pair, Share,' for example. Here, each student in the pair is given a letter A or B. A and B, individually, have to think of an answer. A must then explain their answer to B and then B must explain their answer to A. A and B must then share their answers with the class. Using this strategy, both students are required to come up with an answer, tell each other and then tell the class. No-one gets to opt out of the work. If you had simply asked them to work as a pair to think of an answer, it's quite possible that this could have been the work of just one of the students, not both.

Incorporating even a simple strategy like this into your lesson ensures that every student is involved, engaged and challenged. It cuts down the opportunities for poor behavior and instead, as you continue to use it over time, develops students' skills and confidence in helping each other.

It does take a while to embed these strategies into every day practice and for students to gain competency in using them, but once this is achieved, the cooperative behavior enables progress to take place.

A more advanced technique that is an excellent way of developing cooperative behavior to promote learning is the Jigsaw Technique. To explain this let's imagine that we are teaching history, that the question the whole class have to answer is 'Who was the most influential leader?' and that there are 25 students in the class.

In this lesson, the teacher would divide the class into five groups of five. Each group has to discuss five different leaders: for example: Genghis Khan, Julius Caesar, Alexander the Great, Napoleon and Churchill and put them in a rank order of historical influence.

Each student in the group of 5 is given a letter A,B,C,D or E. As soon as each person is given their letter, the class is immediately rearranged into 5 new groups: all the As in one group, the Bs in another and so forth. Each of these new groups will study just one of the 5 leaders with each individual being asked to study a resource or information sheet different to everyone else.

For the first five minutes of the lesson, the new groups have to work in silence as each member works independently to read through their resource sheets and make notes on things they think are important about their leader.

After this, the cooperation begins. In turn, each person has to teach the rest of that group what they have learned about that leader whilst the others listen and make notes.

At the end of this session, each person in the group will have taught and been taught by the others about this one particular leader. None of the things they have learned will have come from the teacher – it will all have come from each other.

When this stage of the lesson has ended, the individuals return to their original groups where you will now have five students, each of whom is an expert on a different leader. Their new task now, working from person A through to E, is to teach the rest of the group what they have learned about their leader and for the rest to make notes on what the others have said.

At the end of this exercise, each group will have learned about all five leaders and will be in an informed position to debate which leader should be put in which order.

Try to imagine what an observer would see about the higher level behavior in this lesson. From a starting point of total ignorance each student learns about five important leaders and, by the end of the lesson, is able to make evaluative judgments about their importance. This has been done without any 'from the front' teaching but from the participation of all students.

The Jigsaw Technique can easily be adapted for all kinds of subjects and you can play around with group sizes and numbers of groups to match the size of your own groups.

There are many different types of cooperative strategy (including the well-known Kagan Structures) and, depending upon the content of your lesson, there is bound to be one which can be useful.

Remember, of course, that you can't expect students to become skilled in participating and cooperating overnight. You need to keep using these strategies over and over until those skills are embedded and honed.

2)   Giving students responsibilities

We give students responsibilities all the time. Every time we ask someone to hand out books or go on an errand to another teacher we are making them responsible for something. However, to make it an effective tool for developing higher level behavior, it needs to be formalized in your classroom.

This means doing several things:

- stop using volunteers and ensure all students are given a role
- create a list of roles and responsibilities you want in your classroom
- explain explicitly what those roles and responsibilities are
- use a rota to ensure everyone has a chance to undertake a number of different roles
- have clear rewards for undertaking the role and clear sanctions for not fulfilling those responsibilities.

There are no fixed rules about what roles you need to have and you can invent your own, though they will fall into two main areas: academic and non-academic. Academic roles might be the roles you require students to do when participating in cooperative group work: decision maker, recorder, speaker, time-keeper, resources manager, fact checker, etc. You can have one of each type in each working group. Non-academic roles might be helping out with jobs. When I have a group working at a large table I always have someone responsible for handing out and collecting in books; another ensures there is enough pens, pencils, rulers, etc.; a third person is there to ensure that rules are followed – keeping discussion to a reasonable volume, gaining the attention of others when the class needs to be quiet. Other children are assigned special roles such as taking messages to another teacher or getting resources that are not based in the classroom.

All these roles come with a very short, easy to understand job description usually printed out on a small laminated piece of card, which tells students the responsibilities that are expected of them.

The benefit of having roles in class is to develop responsibility in the students. It gives many of them a sense of pride and purpose when given a role and when rewarded at the end, even if it's just something very small like a positive behavior point, there is a sense of achievement and a fostering of self-esteem.

More than this, having a role makes them an integral part of the class and thus it develops those skills in working in a group or a team which leads to higher level behavior and improved learning through working with each other.

By rotating the roles around the class, you show that you have no favorites, are fair, that you have the same expectations of everyone and that you give everyone an equal opportunity. You also get the students to learn a variety of different skills from undertaking a wider range of roles.

As a result, you have a much more cooperative group of students who have a mature approach to their studies.

3)   Developing Resilience

With regard to improving behavior, we have to look at developing a student's academic resilience. By this, I mean looking at ways to stop a student from giving up when they find work challenging or in response to poor test results or bad marks.

A typical way to look at this would be to consider two students who both failed a test. The resilient student would pick themselves up, look for help, try to find alternative strategies to move forward and go on to succeed. The other student would regard themselves as being no good, give up trying and possibly end up disrupting the class.

As a teacher trying to move our students to higher level behavior, it's important to develop resilience in all students, especially those who show very little of it to begin with.

How to do this:

- Show examples of people who have constantly failed then achieved massively at the end. There are countless examples out there, a classic one being Einstein who failed his college entrance exam.
- Show your students your human side – what have you failed at over and over before you succeeded? How did you get there in the end?
- Explicitly teach the benefits of failure: we only progress when we fail and learn from it.
- Look at areas in their lives where they already show resilience and ask them to do the same in your lessons. A good way to do this is to ask the class how many attempts they have at completing a level on their favorite computer game. They will soon see that they will go back and play it over and over until they have succeeded. If they get really stuck, they will find out where they are failing and seek help – either asking other players or looking

on the internet for a solution. Can they do this with a math equation too?

- When asking questions of the class, tell them that you always expect an answer but not to worry if it's the wrong one. This way you take away the fear of failure. Once this has happened they will keep on trying.
- Build self-assessment into your lessons so that students can work out for themselves what they have got wrong and what they need to do to progress.
- Provide your students with assessment ladders, success criteria and check lists to evaluate their own work and find out the next steps.
- Reward and praise resilient behavior.

4)   Independent learning

The final skill students need in order to develop higher level behavior is to be able to learn independently. Unfortunately, many teachers think that this just means getting the students to work quietly on their own without talking to others. If all the children have their heads down writing and aren't interrupting anyone else, then they think independent learning is taking place.

Working independently and learning independently, however, are not the same thing. Independent learning is really project management. It requires a student to plan ahead, set goals and targets, be organized and have the necessary resources available to do the work set.

I've always found that technology teachers do this better than most and I always refer to their techniques when showing other subject teachers how to best develop independent learning.

Technology teachers usually call their independent learning a 'project' and this gives the student a sound model to work on.

Projects always begin with a written brief. This outlines:

- analysis of the task to be undertaken
- description of the final piece of work to be completed
- checklist of goals and targets to be completed
- timetable of goals and targets
- list of resources needed
- outline of research that needs to be completed
- information on the presentation of the work

Only once a student has this in place is the project allowed to begin. However, because the brief is in essence a step by step pathway from the start to the end of the project, it empowers the students to work on their own and gives them mini deadlines to work towards as the project takes place.

Independent work in other subjects can be done in a very similar way, whether it is writing an English essay, undertaking a science experiment, creating a composition in music or reviewing a movie in film studies.

Of course, there are times when you will be doing short bursts of independent work during a lesson and will not have time to get the students to create a brief – even a short one. In these cases, it's up to you, as classroom teacher to create a short brief to put on display as in the example below:

You have 20 minutes to complete the following exercise:

- **Write a summary of the passage we have just read. To succeed it must discuss: the main events that have taken place and the characters reactions to those events.**
- **The summary is to be written as a series of bullet points.**

Having the students prepare project briefs for longer pieces of independent work is an excellent way to develop the skills they need for independent working. Depending upon their age, many of them may have acquired those skills already from technology or other subjects that use them. If this is the case, it's simply a matter of transferring those skills from one subject to another.

The other main area for development when it comes to working independently is building a student's concentration levels. Some students may struggle in a quiet classroom doing the same task over a long period. Here you can teach them other skills to help them cope:

- If they are stuck on one particular aspect, take a break and do something else. As an English teacher I often come across students who struggle with the introduction to an essay and can't seem to move on. Rather than waste time rewriting it over and over until it's perfect, I get them to write the next section and return to the introduction in later.

- Get the students to make a mental note of how long they can last without getting fed up. Challenge them to do a minute longer each time and praise them when they do. It's like getting someone to do that extra sit up at the gym.

- Get students to create a success clock, ticking off a box after every 5 minutes of independent work done without losing concentration. Ticking the time box is a way to self-reward and keep an eye on time limits. It also works as a challenge to keep going.

Getting students to be able to work truly independently increases their confidence and motivation. It improves general behavior, but more importantly, it is a higher behavioral skill that is essential in the modern classroom for students to learn for themselves and make progress.

Conclusion

Hopefully this book will have given you lots of ideas about behavioral management in the modern classroom and given you the opportunity to think about how you can use them to improve behavior in your own classroom.

You may not want to use all the techniques I have mentioned in this book and I certainly wouldn't recommend trying to implement them all at once. Depending upon your own needs, start with the ones you think will have greatest impact first and then gradually introduce the others once you have the first ones mastered.

Remember of course, that behavioral management skills take time to acquire and develop and that once you introduce a technique to a group of students it will take time before they fully take it on board and it becomes an embedded part of your routine. Be patient and resilient and things will fall into place.

If I have one piece of parting advice it is this: the thing you must do, more than anything else, is be consistent. Only through consistently applying these techniques will you embed good behavior and maintain it.

Best wishes for a happy classroom,

KJ O'Hara

Other Books by KJ O'Hara

Be Outstanding: How to Achieve Outstanding Lessons Under The New Ofsted Framework (2014)

'Be Outstanding' covers a wide range of techniques that teachers can implement to improve their teaching in order to work towards getting outstanding under the new Ofsted framework.

It gives clear practical advice about what you should and should not do in observations and in your everyday teaching. Suitable for teachers in elementary, secondary and post 16 education; for experienced and trainee teachers; and senior leaders with responsibility for CPD and teaching.

*"**Excellent:** Very concise and full of practical advice. It's given me a much better understanding of the new Ofsted criteria. I would recommend to any teacher."*

John Hopton – Amazon Review

*"**Fantastic and reassuring.** This is a really useful and positive book."*

Ginette Orton – Amazon Review

9 781499 251876